MONSTER MANNERS

At Home

Written by
Charis Mather

Designed by
Amy Li

Library of Congress Control Number:
2024953020

ISBN
979-8-89359-328-0 (library bound)
979-8-89359-412-6 (paperback)
979-8-89359-383-9 (epub)
979-8-89359-358-7 (hosted ebook)

Printed in the United States of America
Mankato, MN
092025

sales@northstareditions.com
888-417-0195

Written by:
Charis Mather

Edited by:
Rebecca Phillips-Bartlett

Designed by:
Amy Li

PHOTO CREDITS
All images are courtesy of Shutterstock.com, unless otherwise specified. With thanks to Getty Images, Thinkstock Photo and iStockphoto.

Cover – mckenna71, Archiwiz. Recurring – xnova, Agafonov Oleg, Omeris. P12–13 – alexdndz, Tartila. P16–17 – Tartila. P18–19 – Ana Risyet.

Monsters know many things.

They know how to do crafts and how to draw...

They know how to sing and how to garden...

But there is one thing that
many monsters do not know...

MANNERS!

Stomp was the loudest, stompiest monster in the neighborhood. He loved to shout and laugh.

Stomp's best friend was Dot. She was the smallest, quietest monster in the neighborhood. She did not stamp and shout, but she loved to play with Stomp.

At the park, Dot told Stomp all about her new house.

"My new house is amazing!" she said. "It has a downstairs and an upstairs. Every room has brand-new carpets that are super clean and soft."

"That sounds amazing," Stomp said. "Do you think it would be alright if I came over to play?"

"Let's ask our parents," said Dot.

Stomp and Dot got out their phones.

"Can I play at Dot's new house, Dad?" Stomp asked.

"Can Stomp come to play at our new house?" Dot asked.

"Yes," said their parents, "so long as you monsters mind your manners."

Stomp looked a little worried.

"What's the matter, Stomp?" said his little friend.

Stomp frowned. "I don't know many manners," he said.

"That's OK," Dot said brightly. "I know all the new house rules. I can teach you!"

Stomp and Dot made their way to Dot's new house.

She opened the door, and Stomp stomped straight in.

"Wait, wait!" cried Dot. "Your feet are all muddy from the park. Monsters with good manners make sure their feet are clean before they come into the house."

"That's a good rule," Stomp said. "That will keep your brand-new carpets clean for much longer. Thanks, Dot."

Dot helped Stomp clean his muddy feet. Once they were inside, Stomp ran up the stairs, shouting out happily.

"Hello, Mama Dot! It's me, Stomp!"

"Shh," Dot whispered. "We shouldn't be too loud when we are inside. Mama usually has an afternoon nap around now, so we should try our best not to wake her up. Monsters with good manners use their outside voices outside and their inside voices inside."

"No problem!" Stomp said in his softest inside voice.

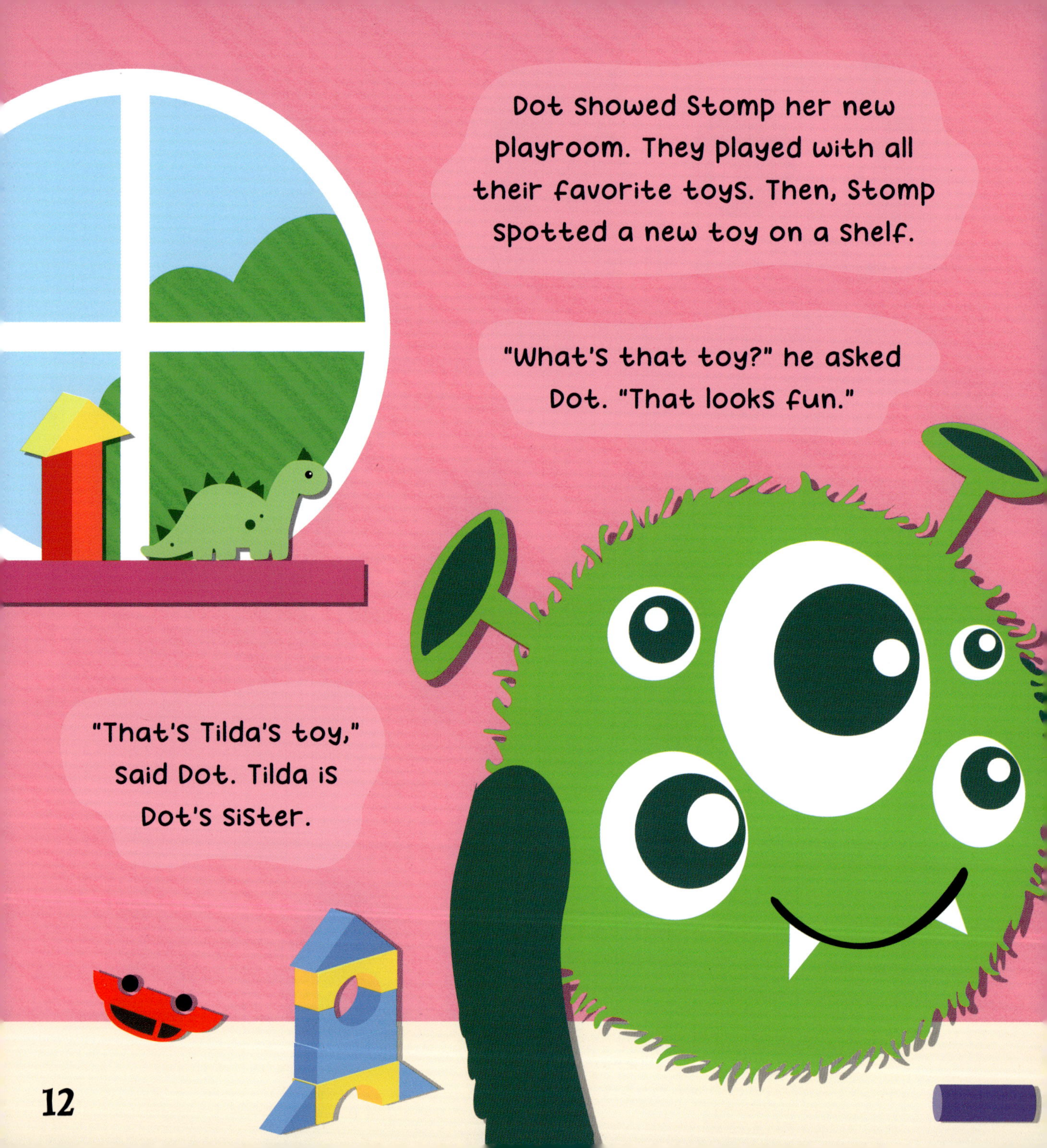

Dot showed Stomp her new playroom. They played with all their favorite toys. Then, Stomp spotted a new toy on a shelf.

"What's that toy?" he asked Dot. "That looks fun."

"That's Tilda's toy," said Dot. Tilda is Dot's sister.

"Can I play with it?" Stomp asked.

"Well, that toy is special to Tilda," said Dot. "She probably won't mind, but monsters with good manners ask before they use other people's things."

"Let's go and ask her, then," said Stomp.

Dot and Stomp made their way to Tilda's room. Stomp started to turn the handle, but Dot stopped him.

"If someone's door is closed, monsters with good manners knock and wait," Dot explained to Stomp.

Stomp knocked politely on Tilda's door and waited.

A moment later, Tilda opened the door. "Hi, Tilda!" said Stomp. "Would it be OK for us to play with your toy?"

"Sure!" said Tilda. "Just make sure you are careful with it. That is my favorite toy."

"We will. Thanks, Tilda!" they said.

Tilda's toy was a lot of fun. Dot and Stomp took turns playing with it until it was time for Stomp to leave.

"That was so much fun," Stomp said.

"It was," Dot agreed. She looked at the toys scattered around the room. "But we did make a big mess."

"We should clean up before I go," said Stomp. "Papa always tells me that monsters with good manners clean up after themselves. That's one monster manner I do know!"

Dot and Stomp got to work putting away every last toy. Stomp took extra care with Tilda's special toy. When everything was back in its proper place, Stomp went downstairs to say his goodbyes. This time, Stomp made sure to walk through the house instead of running.

Dot's mom and sister were in the living room. "Thanks for letting me borrow your toy, Tilda," Stomp said.

"No problem," Tilda replied. "Thanks for asking me first!"

"Goodbye, Mama Dot," Stomp said. "Thanks for letting me come to your new house. I hope I wasn't too noisy."

Mama Dot smiled. "Not at all. Thank you for having such good manners. You are very welcome to come back again."

That made Stomp very happy. "I can't wait." He gave Dot a big hug. "Thanks for playing with me and teaching me so many good manners."

"You're welcome," Dot said.

Dot opened the front door for Stomp and watched him walk down the garden path. When he reached the gate, Dot called out, "Guess what, Stomp?"

"What?" Stomp asked.

"Now that you are not in the house, you can use your outside voice again!" she said.

Stomp grinned. He loved to shout. Stomp took a big breath, waved and in his loudest outside voice, yelled,

"See you tomorrow, Dot!"

Not all monsters have good manners, but Dot and Stomp do. Do you?

Can you remember all the monster manners that Dot taught Stomp?

- Don't bring mud indoors.
- Use your inside voice when you are indoors.
- Ask before using other people's things.
- If someone's door is closed, knock and wait.
- Clean up after yourself.